D1551423

HOW TO FIND
YOUR PURPOSE AFTER 40

The Secret To Unlocking Your Unique Gift To The World

By Susan Paget

This book is dedicated to every brave person who realizes that they are worthy of discovering who they really are. Your journey inspires me

The purpose of life is to live it, to taste experience to the utmost, to reach out eagerly and without fear for newer and richer experience.--- *Eleanor Roosevelt*

The purpose of life, is a life of purpose --- *Robert Byrne*

The purpose of art is washing the dust of daily life off our souls.--- *Picasso*

Be daring, be different, be impractical, be anything that will assert integrity of purpose and imaginative vision against the play-it-safers, the creatures of commonplace, the slaves of the ordinary. --- *Cecil Beaton*

The human race is a monotonous affair. Most people spend the greatest part of their time working in order to live, and what little freedom remains so fills them with fear that they seek out any and every means to be rid of it. --- *Johann Wolfgang von Goethe*

Only I can change my life. No one can do it for me

– *Carol Burnett*

Without leaps of imagination, or dreaming, we lose the excitement of possibilities. Dreaming, after all, is a form of planning – *Gloria Steinem*

"It was my mum who got me into singing properly – she knew I had to do something with my voice" – *Susan Boyle*

Let yourself be silently drawn by the strange pull of what you really love. It will not lead you astray" – *Rumi*

"The thing women have yet to learn is nobody gives you power. You just take it" – *Roseanne Barr*

"I am my own experiment. I am my own work of art" – *Madonna*

TABLE OF CONTENTS

PURPOSE DEMYSTIFIED

Many people think that finding purpose is an incredibly mysterious and magical thing.

It seems to be as elusive as a rainbow and as fleeting as sand through your fingertips. It's like this glittery pixie dust that seems only sprinkled on the privileged, the rich and famous.

But if you look carefully, you'll see it all around and in the most unique (and often amazingly NORMAL) ways. I believe that if we take a moment to really see purpose in all it's forms, not just the one's that we've been programmed or brought up to believe, we can find that unique thing we bring to this world - our purpose.

The general line of thought though is that many of us believe that we have to search far and wide to uncover just exactly what our unique point is.

But here's the truth. I'm seeing time and time again – that our purpose, our whole reason for being on this planet right here and now, is smack dab, right under our nose. We're just so used to ourselves or constantly operating from a lens of self-doubt that it escapes us. Sadly, we're much more apt to admire others and shout their gifts to the rooftops, totally ignoring or putting down what we bring to the "purpose" table.

In this book, I'm going to share with you clues for finding your purpose. The way I see it, purpose is that unique little drop of magic inside of us that no one else in the world has or will ever have. The thing is, clues for this little drop offen get pushed aside for the realities and obligations of life.

I completely get that.

For me, that little drop of magic was also a complete tease, taunting my life, for many, many years. I knew since I was a little girl that I had it somewhere but I could never work out what it was.

By the time I hit my late 40's I was so annoyed and frustrated with my lack of working out what my point was at midlife, that I completely put the brakes on and went on a quest, once and for all, to find it.

Through my experience of soul searching for what it was that made me tick, I've learned a few things about purpose that have been surprising and thought provoking and now I'm going to share what I've learned with you.

FIVE MYTHS ABOUT FINDING YOUR PURPOSE

First off, I think that it's important to start with a few home truths about this purpose thing. In particular, let's talk about what purpose is NOT.

Now, this might **not** be the information that you were hoping to get right away and I totally understand that. I'm going to assume that you probably are in the same place I was when I was actively seeking my purpose. It's a kind of desperate feeling place. You want the secret formula for achieving this now and if you're in your 40's or beyond, like I was when I went on my quest to find it, you're thinking that frankly, you don't have any more time to waste.

But stick with me.

If I would've known some of these things at the start, I might've relaxed a little bit about the whole anxiety provoking aspects of trying to find out what my point was in life. Don't get me wrong, it still would've been important for me to know what *exactly* it was that got my heart beating and what the *unique* gift that I could share with the world was. I just think if I had a little bit of balance on the subject, it might've smoothed my path a little.

So here are the **Five Myths Of Finding Purpose:**

Myth #1 – Finding your purpose means it has to result in you being famous, making heaps of money, and being the next Mother Theresa / Madonna / Oprah / Insert your personal "icon on steroids" here ;)

Myth #1 Busted -

In this day and age, materialism and fame are shoved down our throats from every angle. Even if you don't own a TV or a computer, it's almost impossible to avoid advertising and shopping malls.

On top of that, many of us who are over 40 have been brought up with the idea of success in life meaning financial success. Even though we know in our hearts success can also be the love we have in our lives, the places we've seen and the experiences we've had, subliminally many of us assume that a component of purpose has to be attached to some sort of extreme monetary gain.

But actually, this is not so. Purpose is about contribution and the actual reward is in the giving. Let me say that again because this is extremely important:

"Purpose is about contribution and the actual reward is in the giving".

When a celebrity is monetarily successful, that doesn't necessarily mean they're living their purpose and this would also give a better understanding of the incredible unhappiness that also seems to walk hand in hand with wealth and fame. Fame and net wealth is not purpose. Beginning to let go of the misguided suggestion that purpose equals financial success takes A LOT of pressure off. It completely changes the game of seeking purpose. Now you can focus your energy on the contribution you can make, not the gain.

Myth #2 – You can only have one purpose in life so it better be something so epic that you can stick with it forever and ever and ever.

Myth #2 Busted -

We actually have many purposes in life. Some overlap and some evolve into other things or run their course. Chances are you've already experienced many forms of purpose. For example, a woman who has a child might find one of her life's purposes in being a devoted mother. But then, while she's being a mom, she also knows that she's a writer and she fulfills that purpose at the same time. When the child becomes an adult and leaves, this motherly purpose shifts to her writing full time or heads off in another direction with something else that can be born.

Myth #3 – Your purpose must change the world. It must be something so off the charts that the effect of what you have done will be felt around the globe.

Myth #3 Busted –

Again, like Myth #1 and dismantling the connection between purpose and fame, the idea of living your purpose and changing the world also needs to be adjusted. Take the grand pressure off yourself because the problem is, when we have an insane level of perfection that we expect ourselves to rise to, we often get so wrapped up in fear that we procrastinate to the point of not making a move at all.

The interesting thing though about wanting to change the world with your purpose is that there is an element of truth in the ability to do this and that is the ripple effect of living your purpose. Take the "mother" example that I used in Myth #2. By caring for her child in a loving way, that child would possibly go on to care for others in a loving way, and in turn that love would have a flow on effect.

It would somehow, in it's own gentle approach, change the world. So right now, one of the biggest favors you can do for yourself on your hunt for purpose is to readjust your scale of how it will change the world. I found this idea, of the ability to share my purpose with just ONE person, incredibly uplifting, empowering and ACHIEVABLE!

Myth #4 – Everyone will understand and love your purpose. Your family will be so supportive and happy for you. Your work colleagues and your friends will totally get what you're doing!

Myth #4 Busted –

Not necessarily. There's a good chance that there will be someone or many in your circle who won't understand your quest to find purpose or what you're doing to live it. They might not care. They might even feel resentful. This can feel pretty demoralizing but I've found this to actually be an awesome gauge.

The reactions of others are a litmus test of how committed you are to your purpose. Would you be willing to pursue the thing you feel you are put on the earth to do if the reactions of those around you are lukewarm? Answering "Yes, I would still pursue my purpose regardless of feedback" is a good indication you've found your purpose.

Myth #5 – Finding your purpose is easy! Everyone around who is living theirs seems to have slotted right into it. It's like they knew from the start what their mission in life was.

Myth #5 Busted –

One of the most frustrating misconceptions about finding purpose is that it's simple to identify, activate and achieve. Most of us have assumed that purpose comes easy. But for the majority, purpose is something that needs to be discovered, implemented and doggedly practiced and applied.

Many people will go back to school or find ways to actively train and gain skills to put their purpose out there. I know I did. Those are the hours and years of work that many of us don't see when we admire someone living their purpose. Not knowing that there is often a foundation that needs to be laid for purpose can come as a rude awakening for those who're on the purpose path. The amount of work and energy that's required to live it is often a shock and sometimes the fantasy of purpose doesn't match the reality.

Now that we've got some of the hard cold realities about finding your purpose out of the way (but I'm sure you can see it was worth knowing what they are!) we can move on to the journey of finding it.

EXAMPLES OF PURPOSE ARE ALL AROUND US

In my quest to find purpose, I always wondered if there was some type of formula to get it. For instance:

What roads did people take to find their passionate callings?

How old were they when they knew they had this thing that they had to share with the world?

And what happened - what was the big thing – that propelled them to make a stand and finally go and live their purpose?

I think for any aspiration we have, it's helpful to look at how things have been done before. There's a saying that "success leaves clues" and if there is a particular purpose that you feel driven to pursue, analyzing the steps that a like-minded person you admire took to get theirs can be very enlightening.

My problem was that I really had no idea what my unique gifts were that I wanted to give the world. I just had no context for it. And my bigger problem is that I thought that purpose was wrapped up in Myth #1 – that purpose has to be attached with extreme financial gain. I equated purpose with financial success and because it isn't, that stopped me right there. I could go no further because I couldn't think of one thing I could possibly do that was going to get me to that level.

The pressure of it was too much so I couldn't even get started. I also assumed that purpose had to be some crazy, grand experience and that in itself - having to do something that was going to massively shift my already good life - wasn't something that I wanted to strive for. I loved my life, I didn't want to rock any boats and change things that much.

I just wanted to ensure I was playing with a full deck and that I was bringing my best to every aspect of my life.I felt like once I had that going on then things would settle into place – I would work effortlessly and wouldn't worry that I was letting time pass by because I was living my full potential.

For you, the search for purpose might be tied into being a better provider for your family or making a complete change in your life. We all have our different reasons for going down this path. But losing the shackles of expectations of what purpose should look like is a very important part of just getting started on finding it.

For me, actively seeking my purpose was a long three year search (which honestly would've been shorter if I would've been aware of the ideas in this book.) Eventually though, this search revealed that "thing" I mentioned earlier - that was right under my nose and I learned that my purpose is to help women over 40 navigate midlife and beyond. And the one thing that really stands out about my experience is that I have an understanding of how profoundly personal and "normal" purpose is,

I'm aware that it's not so much this unattainable thing, exclusive to the lucky. It's really just a drive that courageous people have that compels them to acknowledge and nourish what gives their life meaning. If you look around, you'll see someone every day in your neighborhood, maybe under your own roof, living their purpose.

EVERYDAY PEOPLE, LIVING THEIR PURPOSE

Let me tell you about a recent week where I really got that people living their purpose were all around me once I knew where to look for them. In just seven days, I had three profound brushes with people living on purpose from all different walks of life and in turn, their purpose, inspired my purpose – which is to communicate, do so in my unique style and above all, help others.

Let's just pause for a minute and look at what I just said because it is actually a bit of gold:

"My purpose is to communicate, do so in my unique style and above all, help others"

This line is very important. My personal purpose can actually be used as a template for yours. It will REALLY help you when you think about how to articulate your purpose. In fact, there is possibly only one word that you'll need to adjust to personally suit you and that's "communicate". I'm a communicator. That's what I do. What you do might be completely different. So I'm going to leave this word blank but the rest of this sentence will most likely be how you will explain (even to yourself) what your purpose is.

My purpose is to _____, do so in my unique style and above all, help others.

Don't worry if you can't fill in the blank word just yet. You're only getting started. But that line, once you find your "word" is going to sum up what your purpose is. And it's a very powerful line. When I say it for myself, and I say it often, even now, it makes me feel very secure and more committed to what I'm doing.

So this leads me to:

THE FIVE TRUTHS ABOUT FINDING YOUR PURPOSE

Truth #1 - Purpose is contagious.

When you encounter someone else living their purpose, they inspire you to live your purpose and in turn you will do the same. You will inspire someone else to live their purpose simply by being an example of someone living theirs.

Now I was telling you before about a week where I had three encounters with people living their purpose and what unique forms they took. This particular week happened around Valentines Day 2013. But now that I think about it, these kind of examples happen EVERY week, it's just a matter of awareness. While you read this, consider how your past week was and what evidence of purpose you encountered.

First off, the week began with me doing a very weird thing. On my YouTube channel I do a weekly vlog, on a bunch of different topics of interest to women over 40. But on this particular day I happened to be very inspired by two things. First off I was inspired by Valentines Day, but not for the reasons you might think. You see, I'm one of those people who doesn't really get into Valentines Day.

Don't get me wrong, I love romance. I've been happily, romantically married for 30 years. I think romance makes life beautiful and of course I love flowers and chocolates and all the goodies that Valentine's Day can be about. That said, I just never have bought into the whole commercial aspect of it. I'm not a fan of the idea that we're supposed to turn on the charm on one day of the year. To me, love is a 24/7 thing.

So, the vlog began as kind of an anti-tribute to Valentines Day and then evolved into something that really inspired me. On this particular Valentines Day, there was a global event called One Billion Rising. One Billion Rising was created by the feminist playright Eve Ensler who uses her creative skills to highlight injustices towards women. In this event, Ensler and her network asked one BILLION women to come together and peacefully protest the current statistics which reveal that one in three women will be raped or beaten in her lifetime –horrific, right? But rather than fight this with anger, Ensler suggested that this outrageous statistic be countered with the joy of one billion women dancing. And from that, the idea of gathering one billion women to dance as a message on Valentine's Day was born.

Well when I heard about this sublime initiative, I was so inspired. Here was a woman, who had started a movement that touched people right at their heart. And how easy would it be to just swing my hips and bust a few moves in the name of lending my heartbeat to this event. That's all the organizers of the even asked women around the world to do. To just dance – either as a group or on their own. I knew that I would probably come off as an idiot, but there was something in me that was so moved by Ensler's purpose to make the world a better place and the billions of other women who were in turn inspired by her, that I realized I just didn't care how I came off and I started dancing.

So I went and I danced, and I was really excited. I thought it was super fun and I felt empowered by it.

And then I posted it on my social media feeds and I started feeling like, "Oh my God!" "What the hell have I done?" "What if my kids see this or my husband sees this?"

But you know, something that helped me get over that? It was **knowing** that my purpose is to help by using my creativity and my (often wacky!) unique style. It's straight from that line before that I told you to embrace as your own. It's something I know and can do without any resources other than my brain, my voice and my body. I needed to throw embarrassment caution to the wind and feed my purpose. I needed to help others and this was my own way of how I could do it.

Erik Erikson, who was a developmental psychologist came up with very brilliant theories of the stages of our life. He described midlife as a time where we can experience generativity – a time of regrowth and renewed creativity as well as an opportunity to purposely choose how we're going to behave in the world. It's like we've come to some big time fork in the road where we have some serious decisions to make such as:

Are we going to choose to use our life as a tool for leaving the world a better place?

OR

Are we going to opt towards living a life of stagnation – a time where we choose to wilt on the vine and let everything pass by?

So fulfilling my purpose on this one particular Valentine's Day, came through something that practically landed in my lap (or to be specific, something I caught on Twitter) and was inspired by Eve Ensler - a woman who fully lives her purpose. I simply lived my purpose by doing something that took advantage of my communication skills in my own unique way and in a way that helped people.

Which leads me to another truth about finding purpose:

Truth #2 – Finding and living your purpose might result in you doing things that are just plain wacky and nuts!

My dance convinced me that sometimes living your purpose means putting yourself out there. It means taking a stand. It would've been a *million times* easier and safer to *not* dance and to not post it on YouTube. But I'll bet I made at one person smile. I'll bet someone who saw that video thought "If that woman can do this crazy thing because of something she believes in, I reckon I can also do this one crazy thing that's been on my mind".

During my week of seeing purpose when I started looking for it, a person in my circle passed away. It would be my second encounter of what purpose can look like.

And it was through reflection before and during his funeral that I realized that one of the things that I really admired about this person is that he lived dual purposes, loud and proud.

He was dedicated to his work and to his family and through both of these, he was a mentor to nearly everyone who crossed his path. He loved his work – not in a manic and unhealthy way, but as an art form. He loved the materials he worked with and he loved to perfect his art. He loved to share what he learned with others. When it came to his family, at work, he would often talk about them, in fact, his family helped him run his business.

These two passions - family and work - often criss-crossed and they were powerful because they were authentic and ecological – enhancing the world rather than taking anything away from it. He was a humble man who just did his thing, acting out of purpose and it benefited everyone around him and beyond. Perhaps there are those that live a life purpose that benefits many, but destroys the people around them, completely fine to leave destruction in their path, all for the point of living their purpose. That kind of purpose is NOT what I'm talking about here. I'm not even clear if that is truly living on purpose. What I believe about purpose is this:

Truth #3 - Purpose needs to be sustainable and ecological

When we have a passion, something we feel we're destined to do, it's easy to be so fueled on the adrenaline of the idea- which can only last so long- that it inevitably burns out before you get started. To truly live your passion, finding a way to live it, in a sustainable way, that will still be with you the next day and beyond, regardless of how weary you are, is a road to living and delivering true purpose. At the same time, living your purpose should eventually be like sunshine to a seed when it comes to the people around you.

As mentioned earlier when we spoke about the myths of purpose, not everyone will "get" what you're on about when you're seeking or even living your purpose, initially. But when you are "being the change" that you want to see, others will feel the positive effects of that. They will directly benefit from you living your truth, in a gentle, steady way.

The third person I encountered on my week of consciously observing living a life of purpose was my own mother. My mom, who is in her mid 70's grew up on the conflicting border psyche of "a women's place is in the home" and "burn your bra". She had dreams and aspirations that she put on the back burner to raise a family. One of those passions was for her art. She had painted before I was born but for her own reasons, the easel never came out again, until a few years ago. She is now painting (and selling) her art.

And this brings me to a very important truth for those of us who are at the crossroads of midlife and feeling anxious that we haven't found our purpose yet:

Truth #4 - If you're not sure what it is, purpose will wait for you.

Yes, we know that life just zips by and that in the scheme of things, life is short. But purpose can evolve organically. It can appear when the time is right for you. Perhaps, for late bloomers, there's a point in the waiting as purpose simmers, brews and evolves. Perhaps your purpose is relying on time to gain a true understanding and depth. Perhaps for artists and philosophers, purpose needs life experience material in order for it to come alive.

Of course, the challenge is to not let this sit inside you and wait until it's too late to activate it. It's a fine dance of playing with the idea of time and space having no importance and knowing when to bring your passion to the surface. Nurture that spirit inside you, quietly tend it like a little secret garden and then when you are ready, like my mom was ready, you can begin to let the sun of others shine on it. The main thing is to know the difference between the time being right and the fear of holding back from putting your dreams out there.

In fact this is another important question to ask yourself about doing the "thing" that is uniquely you and that is asking:

What is keeping me from living my purpose?

If your answer revolves around fear as in "I'm afraid to leave my job" or "I'm afraid of what others will think" you will be able to see that a barrier between you and going after your purpose is fear.

ARE YOU AFRAID TO LIVE YOUR PURPOSE?

Fear is something that the majority of us have been trained to avoid at all costs, even at the price of living uncomfortably. It's actually almost impossible for us to avoid the feelings of fear because our bodies are hardwired to alert us for any potential threat. The amygdala, an almond shaped region in the brain and among other functions, detects potentials for pain or anything unfamiliar and then sends out the signals to the rest of the body to get our attention – literally that "ick" feeling of fear – whether it means feeling sick to your stomach or tight in the throat and chest and all the other ways fear makes it's physical presence known.

Even if we come from the safest environments and backgrounds, there is deep evolutionary memory embedded in this region. You can pretty much say that seeds of fear were planted from even well before our caveman brothers and sisters when they hid from dinosaurs. So these feelings of built in anxiety are deep.

And all this time later, we still tend to feel fear on a physical level and just the sensation alone can create a knee jerk reaction that makes us either catatonic and unable to make a move or retreating all together.

The fantastic thing is that we're now learning new ways of processing the concept of fear. You can actually see it all around you. Why can one person happily jump out of a plane, even though they've got butterflies, where another won't even get on a plane to travel because the idea makes them feel physically sick? Why can one person throw up before they give a speech (and love every second of being on stage) when another would rather die than do public speaking?

The answer lies in the interpretation of the feeling. Sherold Barr, a life coach, has a perfect way of reframing the idea of fear and that's by considering it as "rocket fuel" - a high octane motivator that will help you with whatever you are trying to do.

In terms of purpose, where fear is keeping you from moving forward, reconsidering it as "rocket fuel" is a powerful way to make the adrenaline, heart pumping byproduct of this emotion work FOR you, not against you. In fact, even understanding that fear was often a "feeling" that could be addressed, accepted and then pushed through anyhow can be a massive light-bulb moment.

Once you're able to work out whether fear is an obstacle to fulfilling purpose, another very strong indicator for determining whether the timing is right to pursue your purpose, is considering the end of your life and whether you could reconcile the idea of not having moved towards it.

There's an awesome quote that's been used by motivational speakers from the self-help guru Wayne Dyer (he actually wrote a book about this exact subject with his daughter Serena) to the Australian football coach Wayne Bennett which says: "Don't die with the music still inside you".

Of course they're not literally talking about music – they are just talking about that unique "song" that only you can "sing". And so this leads to the powerful exercise that can really help you consider whether now is the time to go after your purpose and that is to ask a simple question:

"If you died tomorrow – would that music still be inside you?

If the answer is "I don't know what that music is yet, then that's okay. It will find you if you're willing to keep listening for it. But if you know full well what that music is but you're keeping it under lock and key until the "right time", or until you feel less scared to reveal it, the confronting idea of being at the end of your life and not acting on it might be enough to change your mind and get started.

That Valentine's Day week of observing three people – a stranger, a colleague, and my mother - who had touched my life living their passions and purpose got me thinking about my own journey – one that was loaded with incredible gifts and yet, many frustrations.

If I knew now what I knew then, what would've been different?

The one thing that clicked for me, that brought it all together came back to one simple truth.

Truth #5 You are living your purpose when you serve.

Living your purpose isn't about getting. As much as it would be exciting and fun to assume that once you live your purpose, it gives you heaps of fringe benefits, the reality is in the opposite. What I've found is that living my purpose actually means giving. Helping. Serving.

The more I give – the more I get. It is the universal law that many of us expect to happen the opposite way. How many times have we said, "If I get this (a partner, a job, a baby, a house, a better figure) I'll be able to be happy and fulfilled."? In reality though, purpose goes like this "If I live my purpose and help others, freely, because it feels so good, that will be enough."

For so many years, the idea of this truth was completely lost on me. I sometimes wonder, what would I have done if I knew that purpose had nothing to do with success as we often define it in the Western world? It has nothing to do with material gain. Yes, some people find their purpose financially supports them and that is great. But that isn't the golden rule of purpose.

Where purpose does support you is mentally. It's a place to come home. Purpose is like mental cushioning that gives you peace of mind.

This is priceless. It lets you once and for all, finally know the one main thing that you've always wanted to know about your life is being fulfilled.

Finding your purpose – and living your purpose answers life's big questions. The questions that kept me up all night many times in my life like:

Why am I here?

What's my point?

At midlife I was finally able to answer those questions that I'd wondered (and stressed over) my whole life. I was so worried that I'd go through my life, never getting to the bottom of this deep question.

But learning these truths of purpose, as well as stumbling through the myths showed me even further how much the journey of not knowing was worth it. It made me dig deep into who I was and continues to do so.

Looking for your purpose will do the same. You will really know yourself if you look for your purpose. There will be a part of you that wakes up, that does things you never imagined you'd do. And that's because purpose gives you courage. Fueled by a need to give, just for the sake of giving brings out strength and energy you never knew you had.

Purpose is not time sensitive, but because of our wisdom and the benefit of knowing ourselves for many years, midlife is the perfect time to go and seek it.

THE PURPOSE EXERCISES

.

In this section we're going to go through some specific exercises that are going to activate ideas that will lead you to discovering your purpose. You're going to need a pen and paper – and I suggest getting a journal that you can keep in your bag specifically for brainstorming and daydreaming whenever ideas come to you.

What I love about having a journal with me at all times is that it gives me something to do when I feel stuck and I'm by myself. A lot of times we get so busy being with other people that it's easy to let distractions and putting other's interests first keep us from honing in on our own. So having a journal or something personal to write in is great because there's something about the physical process of writing – good old school writing! – that activates more "under your skin" processes. Research that has explored recall, academic performance and even goal-setting also is substantiating the concept that handwriting has more benefits than banging out words on a keyboard. Physically, writing activates the reticular activating system of the brain which basically filters information. Once this system is initiated it triggers a signal to the cerebral cortex to pay more attention.

For all the science, I think there's something just earthy about actually handwriting – especially when it comes to very personal stuff. I tend to feel actually writing gets to the heart of what you want to do on a metaphysical level and that's the point of what this work is all about - to feel it deeply, personally and let it really become a part of you. I also like the opportunity for you to get away from your computer as the computer in itself can be massively distracting and un-motivating when you're going through a time where you need to dig psychologically deep.

Just take the concept of writing versus typing on board as a way to approach doing the exercises we're about to explore in this book. There's no right or wrong way of doing them though – the main thing is to just get started. If handwriting offers up obstacles, absolutely use your phone or a mobile device, but basically, whichever you choose, have something close by you and portable so you are able to journal anytime and anywhere.

Earlier on I mentioned that most of us don't realize that our purpose and what our point in the world is, is right under our nose. We usually go on this wild goose chase looking for something bigger than ourselves when all along that mysterious thing has been a part of us all along.

The following exercise is an awesome way to start uncovering the aspects of your unique gifts. The best way to consider this exercise is as a bit of an excavation where you're your own archaeologist. Some of the ideas that will come to you through this aren't going to be obvious sources of purpose. You might have to really dig in and extrapolate ideas from them but that's actually the great thing about this exercise because it will have you thinking about all chapters of your life and the possibilities of taking on elements that you hadn't considered before. Don't worry if this doesn't make sense right now. Let's start and you'll understand as we go along.

THE PAST EXERCISES

Step 1. To begin the exercise I want you to go back to when you were around 12 years old. This is generally the time before hormones kick in and we start moving into the socializing rituals of young adulthood. It's an innocent time, a time when, if we're fortunate, we have little responsibility other than functioning in the family, going to school. There are probably things that you enjoyed doing as a 12 year old that were quite unique to you and you might remember specific ways that you would enjoy spending time alone. Think back a bit. What were those things? Really picture them in your mind.

I'll share my experience as an example.

When I was around 12 years old and growing up in San Diego, California, I loved reading. I always had a book going and they generally were series books about girls my age. They were from different time periods like Laura Ingalls Wilder's pioneer stories from The Little House Series or Nancy Drew's "teenager in the 1960's" detective stories or stories of young girls of my generation from the extraordinary author Judy Blume.

Reading about my peers, regardless of what era they were from, was my sanctuary. I just remember feeling so comfortable and satisfied reading these books. It was like being with old friends who knew me so well.

Obviously this time stands out to me so if I was playing archeologist I'd use this as a place to begin an excavation. I would start digging at some things about this childhood experience that really stood out to me - even just playing with words and phrases could provide insight into what my purpose is.

Here are some of the key words and the main ideas that stand out to me:

Reading – Clearly reading was my happy place.

Learning and adventure – I obviously loved learning about people in different time periods, places and circumstances

Stories about lives of girls who were in my age group – All the characters that I gravitated towards were female and around my age group. Even though they were from different times, I really related to the basic and common needs that were specific for teenage girls.

Got the idea?

Now it's your turn to write down what stands out about you as a 12 year old. Put down at least one thought but if you really want to give yourself options to play with, aim for three. Write them down now:

The three main themes of what I was passionate about as a 12 year old are:

1. _____
   _____
   _____
   _____

2. _____
   _____
   _____
   _____

3. _____
   _____
   _____
   _____

Now there's a second step to this where I can then take these ideas even further, brainstorming to a way that resonates with me for where I'm at right now.

Step 2. In this step, I'm going to look at what I've written and delve further. I'm asking myself the questions, "What's the deeper meaning of this word, phrase or idea?" "Do I still enjoy doing this or has this word, phrase or idea manifested in any way through my life?"

Here's what I came up with:

Reading → Enjoyment of language, writing, creativity. This all makes sense to me. I have a working knowledge of different languages, have always written in my career and have always loved the creative aspects of jobs. Reading and writing has always been a constant in my life.

Learning → Curiosity, studying, teaching. This one also made sense to me but in a non-traditional way. I studied yoga on my own for years and often would take classes in writing or practicing Spanish. Most of my learning through the years has been self-taught and I went through most of my adult life thinking that's all I needed.

Stories about lives of girls my age/peers → interest in women's issues, life issues. This also resonated with me. In my adult life I continued to read autobiographies of women, loved stories and information that paralleled my own process whether it was on what to expect when I was expecting babies or on women's wellness, beauty and activism.

Now it's your turn to do Step 2. Have a look at the answers you wrote for Step 1 and ask yourself, "What connection is there between what you loved as a 12 year old and what you've been interested in or not interested in through your life?"

Write down at least three connections, just as I did.

The first connection between what I did as a 12 year old (Step 1) and what I do now is:

_____

_____

_____

_____

The second connection between what I did as a 12 year old (Step 1) and what I do now is:

_____

_____

_____

_____

The third connection between what I did as a 12 year old (Step 1) and what I do now is:

_____

_____

_____

_____

Step 3.

The third part of looking at your past is to see if there are any steps you can take to <u>physically investigate</u> these clues further. So this next step is about taking some sort of action on your clues.

For my example, the action that I could derive from them could look like this:

Reading -> Writing -> I could find ways to read and write for the pure sake of enjoyment, the kind of enjoyment I had when I was a young girl and wasn't thinking about work. The actions I could take could be to start a blog or keep a journal.

Learning-> Studying -> There are some short courses and some different trainings that have sounded interesting. I've also thought about maybe going back to school and studying something that has nothing to do with my career but something I have a passion for.

Stories about life of girls my age/peers → interest in women's issues -> I've seen some organizations for women that sound interesting – like a women's hiking group or maybe volunteering in a situation that helps new mothers or women at risk.

Now from just looking at one aspect of your past (all you need is one, but maybe you have A LOT!) you can get some very strong direction of paths to go down. These are pathways to areas that give you passion and while they might not initially show you how you can live your purpose, you'll find that if you're willing to explore these paths, you'll be more aligned with doing things that give you joy, which will in turn allow you to give more of the innate gifts you already possess and then, it can offer you a surprising pointer to the purpose that is right under your nose. This Past Exercise pretty much operates on a domino affect – one chip leans on the next until they all fold over – click, click, clicking until you end up somewhere…

Now it's your turn to do Step 3.

Write down what kind of present day action(s) you can investigate or consider based on the first two steps. Again, put down at least three actions just like I did. And of course, if you have more than three actions you can take – go for it!

I could:

_____

_____

_____

_____

I could also:

_____

_____

_____

_____

And I could:

_____

_____

_____

_____

Step 4. You'll see that by going through the three steps. you've identified some great information that is very much within you. It's like a message in the bottle sent from your 12 year old self. Now it's time to make good on the promise of your early years. I want you to list at least three things you can do within the next 24 hours to follow up on it.

So when I was seeking my purpose, this is what I did.

1. I made a phone call and signed up to go back to university and do a degree in psychology.

2. I started researching, interviewing and writing about what I was going through as a women experiencing perimenopause. (Note, I still had no idea at the time that I would be doing this as a career, I just was following the direction of what I loved as a 12 year old, reading and writing about girls my age.)

3. I joined a group of women who hiked in my neighborhood.

As you might discover, this is a very powerful exercise for getting on the road to purpose and I still, to this day, marvel at the answers that have come from just sitting quietly and thinking about myself as a 12 year old. I feel like following the guidance of these clues really honors the promise of that young girl. Any frustration that I had about finding purpose really pales in comparison to the idea of not getting reacquainted with her. It is so worth the journey and if you spend time on it, and really think it through, this Past Exercise really activates the "unique" part of your purpose.

THE PRESENT EXERCISES

Once you've worked out some direction to follow from your past, you can move on to the present in your life. The present is what's going on in your life right now and our focus is on two aspects, your "unconscious practice" and "your greatest challenge".

Your Unconscious Practice

The first point of focus is your "Unconscious Practice" – the unconscious practice is the thing that you do that:

You're really good at (even if you don't think so, but others say so).

You don't even think twice about doing.

Other people really might not be good at or don't even try or don't really like to do because it's hard / boring / not their cup of tea / etc.

Chances are you don't really put much value on this "thing" because you do it so very effortlessly, don't attach any importance to it and maybe it just isn't really that glamorous. It might mean that you're a whiz with numbers when everyone else's eyes glaze over or that you know how to cook a mean birthday cake that absolutely delights everyone you make it for. It might mean you have an extraordinary green thumb and can simply look at a plant and it explodes in bloom. It might mean that you love to go for long drives or you're an excellent communicator on Facebook.

For me, that thing that I did all the time without really thinking is that I practice yoga. It's a nonnegotiable part of my life, much like brushing my teeth. I practice when I don't feel good, when I travel, when I'm happy or sad. It soothes me, settles me and is simply a part of my daily ritual. I've done it for years and I do, pretty much without thinking. It's an "unconscious practice".

So here's the big questions. What is your "unconscious practice". What do you put effort into doing on a regular basis simply because you need to. Ironically, you might actually have to be a bit conscious with this when trying to work it out because it could be one of those things that's soooooo normal to you, you can't even detect it.

For example if you're a total neat freak and love to be organized, that might float below the radar and not occur to you that not everyone is like that. Or you might religiously buy yourself flowers every week to the point of often thinking about "What would look nice?" and "What's in season?" and "Where should you place the vase?" when others just work out that they might buy a bunch when they see them. So really think and if you have trouble coming up with anything, ask someone who knows you well.

When you're ready - write down what your unconscious practice is here:

My unconscious practice is:

_____

_____

_____

Now for the next part of The Present Exercise we're going to take the same approach that we took on The Past Exercise and expand on what we uncover.

I want you to take your "unconscious practice" and explore all aspects of what it means for you and what you can do to nourish and explore it further. Using my example, expanding on why I love to do yoga, how I can nourish it and explore it further, I could write something like this:

Practice yoga ->I like to move. I like quiet, I like to focus, I like to hang with other yoga students, I love to travel to India and study eastern philosophies. I could do a teacher training class, I could use my writing skills (see the link to The Past Exercise?) and write articles for yoga magazines or yoga blogs. I could join a new class where I could learn even more about yoga, I could get some books and read more about yoga (which again also takes advantage of my past passions), I could go to India and study there (again, taking advantage of the past passion for learning that I identified earlier)

From this present "unconscious practice" I've identified several ways I can take action on yoga right now! (And actually I did just that as I was uncovering my purpose. I wrote several stories for yoga magazines).

The point of examining this thing that you do almost without thinking is that clearly there is some aspect of passion involved in it. There is something under your nose here that you do almost automatically and chances are there is some element in there that is going to lead you to your purpose in life.

This is a good place to bring up the fact that sometimes these "discoveries" are not literal. For example, I really didn't want to be a yoga instructor, at least not at the time (however, as time's gone on, this might be something I'll do in the future, simply because I might want to share it - which makes me think that there's a bit of real life fortune telling when we investigate our passions). I also had no desire to be a full time yoga writer. When I first really honed in on my "thing" for yoga, I expanded on what rested inside my "unconscious practice" that could be drawn on.

And here's where the "don't be literal about what you do" comes into play.

For one thing, yoga made me *very* disciplined. I'd been doing it for years. At the very least, I knew that I had fortitude and a steady nature and that I was willing to take time and go on a path that wasn't a quick fix in order to find purpose. I also knew that there were a lot of ways to practice yoga and that one of the ways is through service to others. There actually is a school of yoga that is all about volunteering and expressing love! It isn't just about bending into *Cirque Du Soleil* poses. These non literal discoveries would prove very key to what my purpose was as doing something with my life that helps another person is for sure part of it. So deconstructing my "unconscious practice" of yoga and what it meant to me was an extremely valuable exercise when looking for purpose.

So what are several ways you can take action on your "unconscious practice"? List at least three here:

1. One way I can take action on my unconscious practice is:

_____

_____

_____

2. Another way I can take action on my unconscious practice is:

_____

_____

_____

3. And one more way I can take action on my unconscious practice is:

_____

_____

_____

_____

YOUR BIGGEST CHALLENGE

The second part of looking at the clues that the present gives to your purpose is by examining your "biggest challenge".

This biggest challenge is generally not too hard to find because it's when we go through it that we tend to ask purpose questions like "What's going on with my life?" and "Why am I here?" and "What's the lesson in this hell that I'm going through?". It's our big challenges that often take us to task and make us ask the bigger questions which in turn give us a compelling need to find our purpose. The big challenge can prove to be one of our most powerful gifts.

My "biggest challenge" was the fact that I was stuck in a job, that I'd been doing pretty much all my adult life, and it was heading in a direction that I didn't feel good about. In fact it was bringing out the worse in me, not to mention making me sick. I knew I had to work. I actually enjoyed working but that I was doing something that wasn't "me" and didn't seem to be using my talents or energy in ways that I felt good about was demoralizing. I was also really worried that at midlife, it would be hard to change careers – I really didn't know how to do anything else - and because I was mindful of what everyone seemed to think about getting older, that my options were shrinking with each passing month. I felt daunted by the idea of starting all over at such a late stage in my life and worse, even if I was willing to do something I didn't know where to start! I also felt incredibly alone because no one was talking about midlife issues let alone life purpose. I was an outlier to the max!

I didn't realize it at the time but the more I followed aspects of my purpose, like what we're doing here, the more I saw that the EXACT thing that was causing me so much angst – midlife, the silence around perimenopause, starting over, finding purpose, women's issues over 40 and making big change – we're actually what would become part of my purpose driven career of helping women at midlife.

So in this part of examining the present, you want to really have a deep look at what your challenge is. If you're at midlife, it's very common to have relationship challenges or feel disconnected from your body. You might be facing empty nest or contemplating not having children at all. All of these issues bring up thoughts of purpose, of big questions like "Who am I?" and "Why am I here?". Sometimes we loop out on these dilemmas, just thinking of the problem over and over but not looking at how we can actually change things or what advice we would give others in the same situation. But now, this is a chance to put laser focus on to it. No looping.

So right here – I'd like you to sum up your current biggest challenge in just a sentence or two. Do that right here:

My biggest challenge is:

_____

_____

_____

And now, have a look at this challenge and brainstorm on a minimum of <u>10 things</u> – that's right, 10 things you could do with this challenge.

Don't freak. They don't have to be grand things and they don't have to be practical things. Just consider them ideas that will help get your creative juices flowing. So using my situation of being stuck in a dead-end career, here were 10 things I could do with that challenge:

1. Get a coach to help me work through them

2. Put an ad in the paper or on Facebook to see if there are any women who feel the same way and want to start a support group – in person or online.

3. Read books on job transition. (I recommend Coach Yourself to a New Career by Talaine Medainer or my own book Be Your Own Change Guru: The Ultimate Women's Guide For Thriving At Midlife).

4. Listen to inspirational podcasts (You can listen to mine on iTunes.

5. Declutter and do cleaning exercises to gain clarity and get rid of anything I no longer needed related to the career I wanted to change.

6. Identify people I admire and talk to them about how they faced challenges of being stuck or read autobiographies of people I admire who've faced challenges and see how they got through them. Success leaves clues.

7. Move my body. Exercise is an awesome way to get energy going, increase endorphins and come up with ideas and solutions.

8. Look at ways I can reeducate myself – either by going back to school in an area I'm interested in or doing a short term course.

9. Find ways to increase my spiritual foundation (more yoga, more meditation, more time in nature) so that I have resources to draw on during a tough time.

10. Ask the people closest to me to tell me what they think I'm good at. They might have job ideas I haven't considered.

From this list of 10 things, I challenge you to choose at least ONE to follow up on.

Chances are you will have several that are doable but commit to just one to start with. The awesome thing about this list of 10 things is that rather than running away and hiding from a challenge, you're facing it head on and this really changes everything. It creates a snowball effect. Also, by coming up with 10 options, you are able to see there is a light at the end of the tunnel. Rather than limitations, there are options, simply by turning challenge into a growth opportunity and brainstorming how to take full advantage of it. Don't overthink your options, just write them down. Even if an option seems crazy - put it down anyway. One outlandish idea can lead to one that makes sense to you.

The 10 things that I can do with the challenge I'm facing right now are:

1.

_____

_____

_____

2

_____

_____

_____)_____

3

_____

_____

_____

4

_____

_____

_____

5

_____

_____

_____

6

_____

_____

_____

7

_____

_____

_____

8

_____

_____

_____

9

_____

_____

_____

10

_____

_____

_____

THE FUTURE EXERCISE

The final part of this exercise is about focusing on your future. To me, this part of the purpose exercise is a total pleasure because it's pure daydreaming. There's nothing in this but what you visualize about doing, seeing, being, experiencing, learning, loving, etc. etc. if there were no limitations whatsoever. By limitations I'm talking money, time, other people's opinions, logistics – anything that could possibly get in the way of your fantasy. When you do the Future Exercise you have an all access pass to create whatever kind of world you want. It might seem like a total indulgence and even selfish to go into this kind of mindset. Most of us are just so busy getting through the day that the idea of thinking about what we really would do if there were no obstacles can be about as foreign as landing in a country you've never heard of before.

So we're gonna break this concept down into a small segment of time. Just one day. Here's how it works:

I want you to imagine what your perfect day would look, sound, smell and feel like. From what kind of bed you wake up in to the view that's outside your window to the food that you'll eat through the day, the people you'll spend time with, the things you'll do, the way you'll look and on and on. What would your perfect day look like?

Write a few sentences. Don't hold back. Bring as much color and sensation into it. Make it 100% true for you. You don't have to wonder if it would work for someone else at this point. This is your little hiding place of an idea.

Let me give you an example of what a perfect day would be like for me if I didn't have any limitations. It would look something like this:

After an awesome night's sleep on the most comfortable bed with the highest quality sheets and flowers by my bed, I wake up completely rested and am in a small quaint European town.

In my own time I walk down a cobble stone street to a local yoga studio and have a pleasant class given by a teacher in their native language which I may or may not understand. It doesn't matter. I have fun, learn a new word and the sun is shining when I come out of class.

Then I stroll back to my little cottage and sit on the balcony overlooking the street with a beautiful espresso and a perfect croissant and some strawberries.

After breakfast, I shower, put on comfy clothes and sit in a strategic writing corner of my cottage where I can see life in the town yet have privacy. This is where I work on my book for a few hours.

After my writing. I go for a walk through the town for a half hour or so, enjoying the weather, moving my body and shaking out the cobwebs from sitting. I go to the local market and buy ingredients for a great lunch to make at home.

Back at the little cottage, I have my lunch as my main meal for the day and either watch a movie or spend time reading. Maybe I take a brief nap, just because I can. When I'm done, it's time for a beauty treatment of my favorite type of facial and a hair treatment – rituals I love to do.

Once these are done, it's time to pack up my computer and find my perfect café. A place where I can have a glass of wine and some cheese and continue writing for a couple hours with other writers. When we're all done, we enjoy a little conversation before I head home early. I take a warm bath with essential oils and candles around the tub while I listen to quiet music. I dry myself in a luxurious extra large towel and then climb into my comfy bed to go to sleep.

That's my indulgent perfect day. You will notice I did not include my husband or family or specific friends in this fantasy. And this was on purpose. For a fantasy, we need to flat out put ourselves front and center because if we don't, we'll adjust the perfect day to accommodate the other person's perfect day as well. Now, in reality, there would be nothing more perfect than sharing this awesome day with my husband but just for the sake of playing with this exercise – an exercise that will help you find your purpose – it's important to just make it about you. We often have very little opportunities to make something just about us, so thoroughly enjoy the opportunity to do this exercise and make it just for you. You'll see soon there's an important reason to do so.

Now it's your turn to describe your perfect day, from start to finish. Write it down now.

My perfect day begins with:

_____

_____

_____

_____

Writing out what your perfect day would be like identifies some very key points about yourself. You get a clear indication of what makes you happy, you'll notice how you would choose to spend your time, what sensory input you need to feel stimulated, what kind of food you have a passion for, what kind of area you'd want to be in. You even have an idea of what would be the perfect way to wake up and go to sleep.

These are all mega clues to what you can activate right NOW in your life. These are clues that serve two purposes. First off they may hold the key to aspects of your purpose and how you would live it. They also give you ideas of ways that you can adjust your lifestyle RIGHT NOW so you can ensure you're actively loving and enjoying each day. With this kind of attitude you're in a much better frame of mind to consider purpose, how you can serve others, and what qualities are uniquely you. When we're feeling limited, we lose energy, we feel like there's no way out or point in going for what we dream of. When we feel like we have everything that we love and need around us, we have more energy and simply put, it puts us in a position of hope, where we can make bold moves and try new things.

So using my example I was able to come up with the following ways I could implement my fantasy "perfect day" into my reality. At the same time, I could also look at this fantasy day and see if there were any clues that could lead me to what my purpose could be.

I could see that a slow morning ritual is a more natural fit for me to feel good. I can work that into my life by having beautiful bedding and being mindful of the routines I do when I wake up. In other words, getting on the computer as soon as I roll out of bed was not my idea of a "perfect" day so maybe this is something I could consider at home and in my real life.

I could see that of all the things that I could choose to do to spend my time, writing was one thing that brings me great pleasure. Writing was clearly something that I needed to be doing with my life. I know that in the past, writing has always been some part of work that I've done but I had often thought of it as more of a tool than a passion. The exercise reminded me that I would need to take my writing more seriously because it definitely was a piece of me that I actually wanted to do, work or no work. There would have to be some connection between writing and living my purpose.

And obviously I love being in different places. I like being in parts of the world where I don't speak the language. So how could I implement this into my normal life? Well, a few ways. I could work this into my reality by learning a new language or I could start planning a trip. I could make sure that I'm watching foreign movies or at the very least I could ensure I've stocked up on reading book with a foreign twist, maybe about expats in another land or maybe even women, my age and stories from their own cultures (another way of honoring and furthering my 12 year old self, right?). Perhaps my purpose also rests in international pursuits and that's a seed I could consider as planted, just by coming up with the realization.

I also realized by looking at this perfect day that my preference in life is not for a lot of noise around me. I like things relatively simple. And that was with every opportunity to have whatever I wanted for my perfect day.

This aspect often surprises people when they do this exercise because many of us assume that if we had unlimited funds and total support of every step we made, we'd do completely insanely fabulous things loaded with excess.

And sure, there are plenty of ways I at least could choose to live large in my fantasy land but when it's said and done, my happy place is a peaceful place. This overall reality is also important when taking note of what makes you tick and what your purpose is. Before I knew about purpose, I thought that it would be an adrenaline filled experience where I'd be burning midnight oil and everything in my vortex would be spinning brightly. But the truth is, my purpose thrives on steadiness and sustainability (the quality that I mentioned when I was talking about the truths of purpose). Of course what's right for me may not be for you so observing the theme and overall feeling of your perfect day is also a fascinating way to uncover what kind of conditions your purpose could thrive under.

So those are just a few ideas of how I could work my "perfect day" into my real life and also sniff out ideas for where my purpose lies. I love this exercise because for those of us who are sensitive about time and worrying that we're running out of it, this gives us an opportunity to stop wasting time. It's an active way we can start bringing more quality into our life, immediately. It's like creating and living on a canvas where you have more control over the paint and color. Can you imagine how it would feel to begin living your purpose when you start from a "perfect" foundation?

In fact, don't imagine any longer.

I want you to write down, right now, what element of your "perfect day" you can move into your every day AND identify elements that could stand for your purpose, or how you would want to live your purpose. Write three ways here:

One way I can have my perfect day right now
is:_____

_____

_____

_____

And another way I can have my perfect day today is:

_____

_____

_____

_____

And a third thing I can do to make today perfect is:

_____

_____

_____

_____

A Vision Board

One of the most powerful – and fun – tools that I've done when working on my future is to create a vision board – basically a piece of poster board with various cut outs from magazines and brochures that appeal to you.

On the surface, a vision board is pretty much what it says - a visual representation of how you want your future to be. But I feel that the true power of a vision board rests in its *emotional* *r*epresentation. The secret behind creating a vision board is that you clarify exactly how you want to "feel". This is really important to note because no matter what we dream about in life, it's really the *feeling* that's attached to the "thing" that we're chasing. If you dream about finding the perfect partner, you might be concentrating on a certain type of person but when you think about it - you're seeking the feelings of love and comfort and safety. If you dream of being rich, you're seeking the feelings of security, happiness and freedom. When we're dreaming of purpose we might be seeking the feelings of confidence, joy and peace.

So the idea of feelings are important to keep in your mind when you're creating your vision board. I find this also makes the exercise so much easier because that way you have much more options of choice when you're paying attention to what image makes your heart beat a bit faster or if something warm and fuzzy pops into your head, versus being limited to strictly basing your choices only on images that catch your eye. They need to "catch" your heart too.

Here's what you need to do this exercise:

*A poster board of any color you love. If you want you can also use a blank journal cover as your base.

*Various magazines and brochures with photos that inspire you – I like to use travel, yoga, surfing and high-end lifestyle magazines. I use magazines that empower me rather than tabloids or those that are purely celebrity driven. You can also use old magazines and brochures – recycling is great for vision boarding. If you can't find pictures that you like, I've even printed pictures from the internet that I really liked and places like Pinterest or Google Images would be an awesome resource for printable ideas. Some people like putting pictures of themselves in their vision board and this can be powerful because you're literally putting yourself into your future. Just make sure that the photo brings up great emotions for you and that everything about it – where and when it was taken, who you were with, etc. – give you feelings of the emotions that you are seeking.

*Scissors

*Glue stick

Once you have all your materials ready, the fun begins. Start looking through the magazines that you've collected and anytime you see an image that gives you a positive emotion of what living your purpose would feel like, cut it out and glue it on your board. See pictures of a person looking like they're doing what they love? Cut and paste! Doesn't matter if you know who they are, if they're the opposite sex or a completely different age group. Cut and paste! See a picture of a place that gets your heart beating with excitement? Cut and paste! The idea is that once you've filled your board with all these images that have strong emotional attachments, you will be able to look at it and immediately feel the feelings of what it will be like to live your purpose.

It would be really easy to discount this final exercise as a silly new age concept but I find that it consistently works. I've made vision boards throughout my journey to find my purpose. They let you aim for the *feeling* of what you want versus literally looking for a certain thing to be. This is especially important as many of us, when we begin the hunt to look for purpose have no idea what it will look like – but when we take a moment and focus on how we want it to feel, on an gut level, we're able to put together a very important piece of the purpose puzzle.

My vision boards totally amazed me and I've heard this feedback from others who've done them. I would make them during incredibly down times and then, as long as I committed to the forward motion from the exercises in this book, when I looked back at them, I realized that many of the feelings that I was after had completely manifested. Not necessarily like the image on the poster board, but the feeling that was intended, absolutely.

I would stash some of those early vision boards in places where no one, including myself, could find them. Even though they're so pretty (something about all the colors and positive images really results in a lovely looking picture) I was kind of embarrassed about being so raw and honest with the emotions I was searching for. So I'd stuff them away. The crazy thing is, even though they were out of sight, when I'd look back at them, I could see that the visions and feelings that I was seeking were either in development or had already happened. It's as if you plant subliminal messages in your brain to say, "Start heading in this direction" and organically and effortlessly, you do.

Making a vision board is actually quite a spiritual project because you're symbolically creating a new chapter in your life – one where you're intending to bring your highest self and potential to. It's fun to create an atmosphere when you do this exercise. Light some candles and put on your favorite music. It's also a great activity to share with a friend or family member. When you're finished, if you want to see it often, put it up in a place where there's joy in your home – on the fridge or in your office. You can even take a picture of it with your phone and use it as wallpaper or add it as a screensaver.

PUTTING IT ALL TOGETHER

Now we're going to take elements of all the exercises that we've done - The Past, The Present and The Future and pull them together to create a blueprint for your own pathway of purpose.

One misconception that might come from a first glance at this book is that because it's small in word count, the actual work aspect of it is also short and therefore, the results are instant. If you've really gone through the past exercises, you'll know that this isn't the case and that the exercises take time and dedication. It might take days or even months to be able to wrap your mind fully around the concepts. This is a good thing. The exercises here are a gift that keeps on giving. I'm *still* looking to my 12 year-old self for clues about how to take my purpose further. It's helpful to think of these exercises you've done almost as meditations that get to the heart of who you were, who you are now and where you want to go. In many ways these questions are the essence of purpose, the difference is that rather than be just questions that swirl around in the back of your mind when you have a moment to think about them, you're actually taking time to investigate answers and directions.

If you found that the exercises revealed very little and that there were no enlightening moments, I'd like to invite you to let them sit for a while before you get to this point to ensure you're ready. There's a good reason for coming up blank. We have to remember that by the time we get to our 40's and beyond, we are often the product of some major embedding of belief systems that told us, since very early on what we needed to do, how things have to be now and the way they're going to go in the future. We really might just not remember what our 12 year old self really loved doing or we might just not be able to envision a perfect day, or at the very least, be able to envision a perfect day that only revolves around ourselves and not a significant other. All of this is perfectly understandable. I also believe that if this is true for you, it's part of the purpose process. It just might take time for some of the ideas to sink in. The timing of this all will be perfect for you. Perhaps revisit the exercises at another time when you've been able to sit with the ideas and things become clearer. You'll know when you're ready to begin.

If you're ready to pull everything together, you're going to need your journal because we're going to go back to the main points you identified in each exercise, beginning with The Past Exercise.

In The Past Exercise, you identified three main themes of yourself as a 12 year old. You'll recall that mine were: Reading, Learning and Stories about girls my age.

Write your three main themes:

1.

2.

3.

You'll recall that in The Future Exercise, we created a Vision Board and the main agenda for that was to find images that cultivated an emotion we desired. Using the same type of concept, I want you to now look at the three main themes that emerged from your 12 year-old self and identify *at least one* emotion that you feel when looking at your three themes.

I'll use myself as the example. When I look at my three main themes, I get a feeling that's a combination of feeling very inspired and being thirsty to learn and communicate. For the sake of writing down one emotion, I'm going to say the great emotion that I feel when I look at the three themes of my 12 year- old self is: Curiosity.

Curiosity really rings true for me. The concept of curiosity makes my heart beat faster and wakes me up better than any espresso. I love entering new worlds whether it's through the written word or an in-person encounter. This emotion resonates with me just as much as it did when I was 12 and my head was buried in a book that I wished would never end.

Without curiosity in my life I'm absolutely parched and looking back, to the times when I was feeling most despondent about not being able to find my purpose, I really was numb to curiosity. The only time I came alive at work was when I was traveling, otherwise, I felt like I was in a cage. It didn't need to be that way but I didn't realize the importance that staying curious had for me. In fact, I didn't think that it was a good quality to have at all because to me it signified a kind of lack of knowledge. My ego was clearly battling to stay afloat in those days.

This realization is very powerful for me and you might have the same experience, that the thing that actually made you feel so happy as a 12 year old somehow got buried and even diminished in importance as time went on.

So, what is your overriding emotion when you look at your three themes? What emotion makes you smile and feels aligned with a part of you right now? It's time to write this down.

The emotion I feel when I look at the themes of my 12 year old self is:

Now we need to sum up The Past Exercise by just pulling what you learned about yourself into one or two sentences. This should include the core elements of what you loved to do and the emotions you feel. It needs to be written in a way that you can apply to right now. You are more than welcome to use my sentence as a template, inserting your unique emotions, etc. in place of what I wrote. Mine looks like this:

"Communication and things that stimulate my brain- whether it's through reading, writing and learning are important to me because they fulfill my need to feel curious."

Write down yours here:

Once that's done, copy the sentence and paste it onto a separate page. This separate page will be where the summaries of all your exercises will be. The end result will be Your Purpose Blueprint.

Next up is to take a look at The Present Exercise. In this exercise you were asked to identify your "Unconscious Practice" - that thing that you do without even giving it a second thought. My unconscious practice was that I practiced yoga. Write down what your unconscious practice here:

My unconscious practice is:

You also identified what your "Biggest Challenge" is. You'd recall that my biggest challenge was that I was going through perimenopause and couldn't work out why I was so ignorant on the subject and that no one seemed to want to talk about it. Please write down what your biggest challenge is here.

My biggest challenge is:

Now I'm going to have you combine both of these answers of "Unconscious Practice" and "Biggest Challenge" into a couple sentences. The aim is to find some way to connect them by making your unconscious practice an action that actively seeks an answer to your biggest challenge. It might sound a little confusing so let me use my example to explain further.

"My unconscious practice is yoga and my biggest challenge is navigating women's health issues. Yoga is about inquiry, discipline and practice and I will use these actions to guide me through learning more about women's health at midlife."

So for example if your unconscious practice is that you love to cook and your biggest challenge is that you want a healthy relationship, you could play with a connecting sentence or two like this:

My unconscious practice is cooking and my biggest challenge is that I want a healthy relationship. Cooking is about sensual pleasure, experimenting and sharing and I will use these actions to guide me in creating a relationship.

It's your turn now to sum up The Present Exercise. Please craft a couple sentences that connect your unconscious practice to your biggest challenge and if you get confused of what to write, don't hesitate to follow the gist of how I wrote mine by using my sentences as a template and personalizing it with the actions that are possible from your unconscious practice to your biggest challenge.

The connection between the actions of my "Unconscious Practice" to my "Biggest Challenge" is:

Once you're done, copy and paste these sentences on the separate page of Your Purpose Blueprint, right underneath where you put The Past Exercise summary.

We're almost there.

We're now going to turn towards the future by looking at your Vision Board and examining your Perfect Day.

First off, revisit your vision board. Pay attention to the colors you chose. Consider the pictures and the messages they give you. My vision board is full of vibrant oranges and pinks, I don't know why other than those colors make me happy. The pictures I chose are of far-flung places with exotic people that activate my feelings of exploration and curiosity.

And when I look at my perfect day, I see my passion for peace and simplicity as well as my desire to write and communicate. Once again, I'm going to connect these two exercises but this time I'm going to use them as a statement about how I will live my life. My statement looks something like this:

"I live a life that honors my curiosity by constantly exploring. I express this curiosity through communicating and I know, to fully nurture and support myself, I need to incorporate peace and simplicity.

You'll see I am thinking about how to really give my emotions a way to be expressed. in my case, writing is a continuous theme in my life and that's how I can honor these feelings. As well, like a plant, I know what kind of "fertilizer" I need to grow my abilities. For me, burning midnight oil and zipping around in a noisy environment isn't conducive to how I can honor these feelings. I know this and I live it. For example, now, as I write this book, I have soft candles on my table. The house is quiet except for some low, mellow music. I actually napped for an hour in the morning before I wrote to settle my thoughts. This is my perfect environment for living my life themes and nurturing the emotions in my life.

And now to you, write down a statement here about the kind of life that you choose to live, how you honor your emotions and express them. Finish the statement by including the type of atmosphere you need to support these emotions. And of course, if you need a guide for structuring your statement, use mine.

My statement is:

Once you have finished this statement, again, copy and paste it below where you posted the summary of The Present Exercise" page.

And last, is that key sentence about purpose that I shared with you at the very beginning of the book. It is the money sentence because it specifically lays out what your purpose is.

My purpose is to _____, do so in my unique style and above all, help others.

You'll recall that my 'fill in the blank" for this sentence was "communicate". My purpose is to communicate, to do so in my unique style and above all, help others".

If we break down this sentence, you'll see that all of the exercises have played a role in what this means. The blank area could be uncovered in the "12 year-old" you, it can be in how you action your "Unconscious Practice" and how you spend your "Perfect Day". Your unique style has been uncovered in your "Unconscious Practice", your "Perfect Day" and your "Vision Board". And your potential to help others definitely can be found in your "Biggest Challenge", your "Unconscious Practice" and even your "Perfect Day".

One thing to note about this final sentence. Filling in this blank bit might be a work in progress. It might not come to you immediately. But living the blueprint will eventually allow you to fill that word in. When you find the perfect word for this blank, you will know it. It will feel as natural as putting on a perfect fitting glove. If you can fill it in now, go for it

My purpose is to _____, do so in my unique style and above all, help others.

Whether you can fill it in now or need more time, copy the sentence and paste it to the bottom of The Future Exercise summary in Your Purpose Blueprint

Your Purpose Blueprint

Now, it's time to have a look at the sum of all the exercises, Your Purpose Blueprint. Mine is below and I have to tell you, that when I read it, it's *not* about fireworks and excitement or bells and whistles. It's pretty much completely the opposite of the type of myths of purpose that I envisioned before I actually went on the quest to find it. In fact, when I read it, it feels like I'm home. It feels like me.

Here's what my Purpose Blueprint looks like:

"Communication and things that stimulate my brain- whether it's through reading, writing and learning are important to me because they fulfill my need to feel curious.

My unconscious practice is yoga and my biggest challenge is navigating women's health issues. Yoga is about inquiry, practice and service and I will use these actions to guide me through learning more about women's health at midlife."

I live a life that honors my curiosity by constantly exploring. I express this curiosity through communicating and I know, to fully nurture and support myself, I need to incorporate peace and simplicity.

My purpose is to communicate, do so in my unique style and above all, help others."

So, have a look at your blueprint. Whether you are able to finish the final line or not, ask yourself if this feels like "home" to you. Home means that actually taking actions on the emotions you need are possible for you to do right now. I know that even if I had no idea what that final word in the last line was, I could certainly pay more attention to my yoga practice and ensure that I found ways to express myself through writing and learning. That is exactly what I did until finally, I realized, without any effort at all, that I was serving and communicating on issues that impacted women over 40. It just happened because it was using every instinctual, natural bit of me. I was communicating, in a way that was uniquely me and if I could help just one person, every day in my own way, then the mission of purpose has been accomplished.

This is the aim of Your Purpose Blueprint. Follow it, even if you're unsure of the direction it's leading you. Because you'll be following your heartfelt emotions and passions, you will soon grow to love the journey, regardless.

By now, you've really done some serious work and I want you to know that by doing these exercises you've immediately put yourself on the path to not only finding but living your purpose. By all means, this is not a quick fix or an easy path. You'll find there are tweaks and adjustments you'll need to make as you forge your way from extrapolating clues and moving forward with them and then road testing what works and what doesn't. But the bottom line is, you're on the road to finding it and there's no turning back. In fact, you're now ready to consider one the final part of seeking purpose. It's one of the most important ingredients in the mix that makes up what you're here to do and that's where we're headed now. Our focus now turns on how we can serve others.

HELPING ONE PERSON DOING WHAT YOU LOVE

When we first started this quest for purpose together, I shared that one of the elements that was completely lost on my when I started to seek it was the idea of helping. I thought I would need to "get" something - in my case, a perfect job - to live my purpose. But I was completely off the mark and knowing this fact will unlock the "mystery" behind finding purpose. What has become abundantly clear as I go down the road of living on purpose is that we are doing it when we're contributing to others – maybe to those closest to us, maybe to our community, maybe to people you will never meet in person. Regardless of how it takes form, living our purpose is about being of service.

It's about being able to answer the question "What is the unique way that I can help others and contribute to making the world a better place?" Remember making the world a better place doesn't have to be a grand statement. It can be the smallest, gentlest gesture that might only influence one person, but ripples on to reach countless.

To unlock out how to be of help and of service, I want you to look back to your biggest challenge. The description you wrote will most likely hold an answer of what your purpose is or at the very least will be another tool to propel you towards your calling. This big challenge, that feels so very personal and difficult, is one that's actually being felt by someone else right now. It might not be the exact thing, and perhaps, like the emotional pull in the pictures of your vision board, it might just be that someone is feeling the emotions of your biggest challenge. But regardless, this is your opportunity to find a way to help someone by offering the kind of comfort that you would seek.

For example, I found that by getting a conversation going about midlife with friends and family and by sharing what I was going through – feelings that I felt there was a strange code of silence about – I was able to give others the opportunity to share their feelings. By me reaching out and sharing my isolation on this subject, I was showing others that they weren't alone. This was an incredibly easy way of using my big challenge for life-changing good. It certainly wasn't intentional at first. It was just pure instinct to talk to others but I soon learned that there was more to it than just having a conversation. I noticed that the more I faced up to my big challenge, rather than running away and hiding from it, I immediately began to feel better. I naturally started to feel, over time, like I was on track, like I was making a difference. Even now as I still follow these principles, I check in with myself and ask "How am I feeling?" And I feel good. I'm pretty confident in saying that I feel better than I've felt in my life. This is big because so many women are told that when they go through midlife and processes such as perimenopause and menopause that they're going to feel terrible. But for me, uncovering purpose and finding ways to serve has been as good as any hormone treatment. I feel more myself than ever. Such is the power of helping others.

As time's gone on and I've become clearer on my purpose, first and foremost on my mind is continually working on ways I can help others. I want to share everything I learn and am going through. Even when there are challenges – like I said, finding purpose isn't a cure all for life's complications. But the bottom line is that I feel this incredible sense of satisfaction. It's this feeling like if it was all over tomorrow, I'd be completely okay because I'm not, as I mentioned in the confronting quotes of "The Present Exercise" going to "die with the music" still inside me. I'm living a life that is continually on point, ticking the boxes of my personal way to live purpose (communication), my unique way of delivering it (my writing, my videos, my podcasts and talking with people) and by helping – even if it's helping one person.

That's the path you're taking on by following these steps. Even when the going get's hard and things feel dark, you'll get glimpses of your truth there.

In fact, I think now is the perfect time to add that if this book has helped you in any way, then I have well and truly lived my purpose and the gratitude to you that I feel is off the hook. Come to my website and send me a message to let me know if it impacts you at www.thechangeguru.net

NEXT STEPS

Although this is the end of this book, you are at the very beginning of an incredible chapter in your life. You're also going to discover that all of this has come at the perfect time and that, like you read before, your purpose has really been there all along. It sometimes just takes observing everything from different angles to be able to pull the pieces all together. I often have described purpose as a set of puzzle pieces and that's really what it is. It takes courage to be willing to put them together and because you've gone through this book, and taken on all the exercises, you'll see that's exactly what you have, by the bucket load.

Because this is really the beginning I want you to have a set of resources that can help keep you going. I have road tested everything whether it's a book I suggest or a method I mention in a podcast.

Of course the book I especially want to recommend is my first book Be Your Own Change Guru: The Ultimate Women's Guide For Thriving At Midlife. This book really goes in depth with how I specifically found my purpose so if you were inspired by the little outline I've given you in this book you'll be blown away by what I share in BYOCG. It also has more great exercises that are actually used by accredited life coaches. This book is really making a difference to women, it's super easy to read and it really is like having your very own life coach at your fingers tips,

YOUR PURPOSE TOOL KIT

The following is a list of resources that inspire me in the area of purpose.

Be Your Own Change Guru: The Ultimate Women's Guide For Thriving At Midlife

This is the book that outlays my whole career transition journey. it will change your life! You can get it on Amazon.

Creative Visualization By Shakti Gawain

This was a very influential book for me throughout my life. It was quite a breakthrough book on the mere idea of thinking about what you want and then creating it.

The Artist's Way By Julia Cameron

If you're a creative who's blocked, you'll find this book an excellent companion for getting unstuck.

War of Art By Steven Pressfield

This is a pep talk, especially for writers and creatives. Also available on audio if you prefer to listen for inspiration.

Turning Pro By Steven Pressfield

If you're feeling insecure about the real job you want to do, this book will guide you to take your dreams seriously.

The Writers Journey : Mythic Structure for Writers By Christopher Vogler

This was my first introduction to the concept of the Hero's Journey and talks you through it from a writer's point of view. Fascinating book that has influenced a lot of my work in the area of purpose.

The Hero's Journey: A Voyage of Self Discovery By
Stepen Gilligan and Robert Dilts

More information on the classic structure that many say
symbolizes a life well lived. This book takes Joseph
Campbell's principles and specifically applies it to how we can
live a more meaningful life.

A Year of Miracles: Daily Devotions and Reflections By
Marianne Williamson
Guidance for looking at your quest for purpose in a spiritual
light based on Marianne Williamson's life work relaying the
spiritual text "A Course in Miracles".

Roseannearchy: Dispatches From The Nut Farm By

Roseanne Barr

The audio version of this book remains a very influential book

to me but was especially important as I was transitioning

careers. Roseanne Barr is one of a kind and this book has

very strong feminist messages. If you like Roseanne, you will

love this book.

Prime Time: Health, Sex, Fitness, Friendship,Spirit –

Making The Most Of All Your Life By Jane Fonda

The thing I appreciate the most about the book is that Jane

Fonda demonstrates that she's able to live a purpose beyond

being an actress and uses that thing that's right under her

nose – growing older- as her inspiration for helping others.

The Change Guru Podcast:I produce weekly podcasts about

all subjects that impact us after 40. You can find out more info

at http://www.thechangeguru.net

Youtube videos: I do at least one video a week on YouTube

that covers everything from motivation to learning to love your

body as you get older. You can subscribe at

http://www.youtube.com/susanpagettv

THE ROAD TO PURPOSE

Before I finish up I want to leave you with a few bits of advice so that you can really get the most out of your adventure towards purpose. And by the way, don't you think it's good to consider this an adventure? Adventures are challenges that must be taken with a mix of preparation and openness to mystery. They are for the brave and generous of spirit. They're hero's journeys with tests, allies, elixirs, thresholds and mentors. So many times we think of finding purpose as a drudge. As a dive into a dark pool of angst when a sly little reframe can completely change the overall way we even approach it.

Again, this is the kind of stuff I wish that I had in the back of my mind when I first started out, but I suppose, like I mentioned in the exercise about "The Biggest Challenge" it's the things that we learn to solve our own problems that are what we can use to help others, and in turn, live our purpose.

What You Put Into It Is What You Get

It's so easy for us to ponder our situations but often so difficult to bust a move to improve them.

This is probably the biggest failure of the self-help movement. Many of us are total experts on theory and approaches to get ourselves out of a metaphysical tunnel but it's in the doing that presents the biggest hurdle. If you're not sure about this, listen to self-help talk radio. Often a caller will go on and on about their problem. They love their problem! But when it comes to the actual rolling up the sleeves and moving towards a solution, they can't seem to get to the start line. I don't want this to be the case for you.

There is no doubt, the exercises in this book are challenging! They will probably push your buttons and uncover some things in your life that aren't working. It might feel like trying to tackle them is in the "way too hard basket".

But I truly believe that just by reading this book and getting to this point, even if you don't do the exercises, some message that I've written is going to change something about your life for the better. Even if it's just the concept that some of us would rather stay in love with our problems, than risk the unknown world of living without them. Maybe that sentence will allow you to question whether you've been holding back from finding your purpose because of the mysteries that are ahead.

But one thing that I know for sure is that if you actually roll up your sleeves and do the exercises you are going to really get the benefits. So the bottom line is your success in finding your true purpose is really dependent on the effort you will put in to moving toward it. I believe in you and your potential so please keep that in the back of your mind should you have any doubts. Someone is out there – ME – thinking about YOU and cheering you on!

This Isn't A Quick Fix

Finding your purpose is an indirect science. It's a life changing experience that will take an indefinite amount of time. Don't rush the process and don't worry if you're making an effort and it seems like nothing is happening. Sometimes it takes a whole host of changes and circumstances to combine to get things moving. It really took me three years to get on track with my purpose and that I suppose is a long time. But the thing is, I don't regret any day spent getting there – even if the steps were incremental, I was moving forward and this is really important for you to keep in mind.

The truth also is that I must continually honor the idea of doing my "thing", doing it in my own unique way and helping others. Purpose needs to be constantly nourished so this is a concept that is all about the journey, not the destination.

It's Okay To Ask For Help

Absolutely ask for help if you get stuck on this journey. Sometimes we think that we're all alone on the issues that are most important to us. So many people want to help you, including myself, so ask for help! And on that note, keep in mind that when you ask for help you actually are giving someone the opportunity to live their purpose. It's great how this all works, isn't it?

What Else Can You Do?

Have you ever thought about telling your story of how you found your purpose? Now, when you're seeking it is the perfect time to start a blog or a vlog or a podcast and share the adventure with others.

What if you create a business around your "biggest challenge" or what if you start a support group for others who share your "biggest challenge"?

What if you drew your "biggest challenge" or learned to express it in music?

These are immediate ways you can help people and do it in your unique way and what I really love about these ideas is that they help us find our inner voice. We learn to say what only swirls around in our brains. Can you imagine how much better you will be in communicating what you want when you are literally speaking your mind? We live in such an amazing time where there are so many great tools for expressing ourselves and sharing our message with the world. Having a play with the idea of being creative with your quest to find your purpose could be your purpose after all.

THANK YOU SO MUCH!

I hope this book has inspired you as much as I was inspired writing it. It's funny because the idea of purpose was such a weight around my neck for so many years, but now, it's completely the opposite. I LOVE talking about how to find purpose and sharing everything I know about it.

So thank you so very much for reading it and spending time working on the exercises. Put this book somewhere where you can access it another time because you can always revisit the exercises or use it as a bit of a pep talk when you feel stuck.

I'd love to hear what you think about it. Come and say hello at my website – thechangeguru.net or my YouTube Channel – youtube.com/susanpagettv, my Facebook page – thechangeguru.net or Twitter @The_Change_Guru.

You can also email me – I read and appreciate every message I receive.

Thanks again for reading and more than anything, thank you for seeking your purpose – the world is absolutely a better place because you are.

Susan Paget

susan@thechangeguru.net

BE YOUR OWN
CHANGE
GURU

The
Ultimate
Women's
Guide
For
Thriving
At Midlife

SUSAN PAGET

Buy the book that will change your mind about midlife –
Available in print and Kindle on Amazon

41256966R00077

Made in the USA
Middletown, DE
07 March 2017